MATHEMATICS AT WORK

Neville Barnard
illustrated by David Stanley

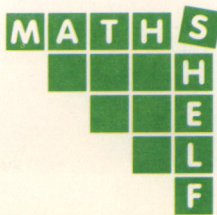

MATHS SHELF

ASHTON SCHOLASTIC
SYDNEY AUCKLAND NEW YORK TORONTO LONDON

Barnard, Neville.

Mathematics at work.

ISBN 1 86388 183 2.

1. Mathematics—Juvenile literature. I. Stanley, David. II. Title.
(Series: Mathshelf.)

510

First published in 1995 by Ashton Scholastic Pty Limited A.C.N. 000 614 577,
PO Box 579, Gosford 2250. Also in Brisbane, Melbourne, Adelaide, Perth
and Auckland, NZ.

Typeset in 19/24pt Memphis Medium and 15/21 Stone Informal Semibold.

Printed in Singapore through Global Com Pte Ltd.

9 8 7 6 5 4 3 2 1   5 6 7 8 9 / 9

If you thought mathematics was something you did at school from a textbook or worksheets, then think again. Come and join two special detectives, Cal Culator and Dee Nominator in their efforts to track down the evil villain, Number Cruncher, as he leads them on a wild trail of mathematical destruction. No person who uses mathematics is safe from his evil clutches. Discover many of the places and people who use mathematics. It won't take long to realise that mathematics is not found only in the classroom.

The villainous Number Cruncher..

makes his escape...

WARNING:

The infamous criminal known as the Number Cruncher has escaped!

He was last seen heading for the corner of Plus and Minus streets...

Keep your eyes open for missing and muddled mathematics.

We find our heroes, Dee Nominator and Cal Culator, on the trail of the villainous Number Cruncher. He is seeking revenge for being put behind bars for fiddling numbers to steal money.

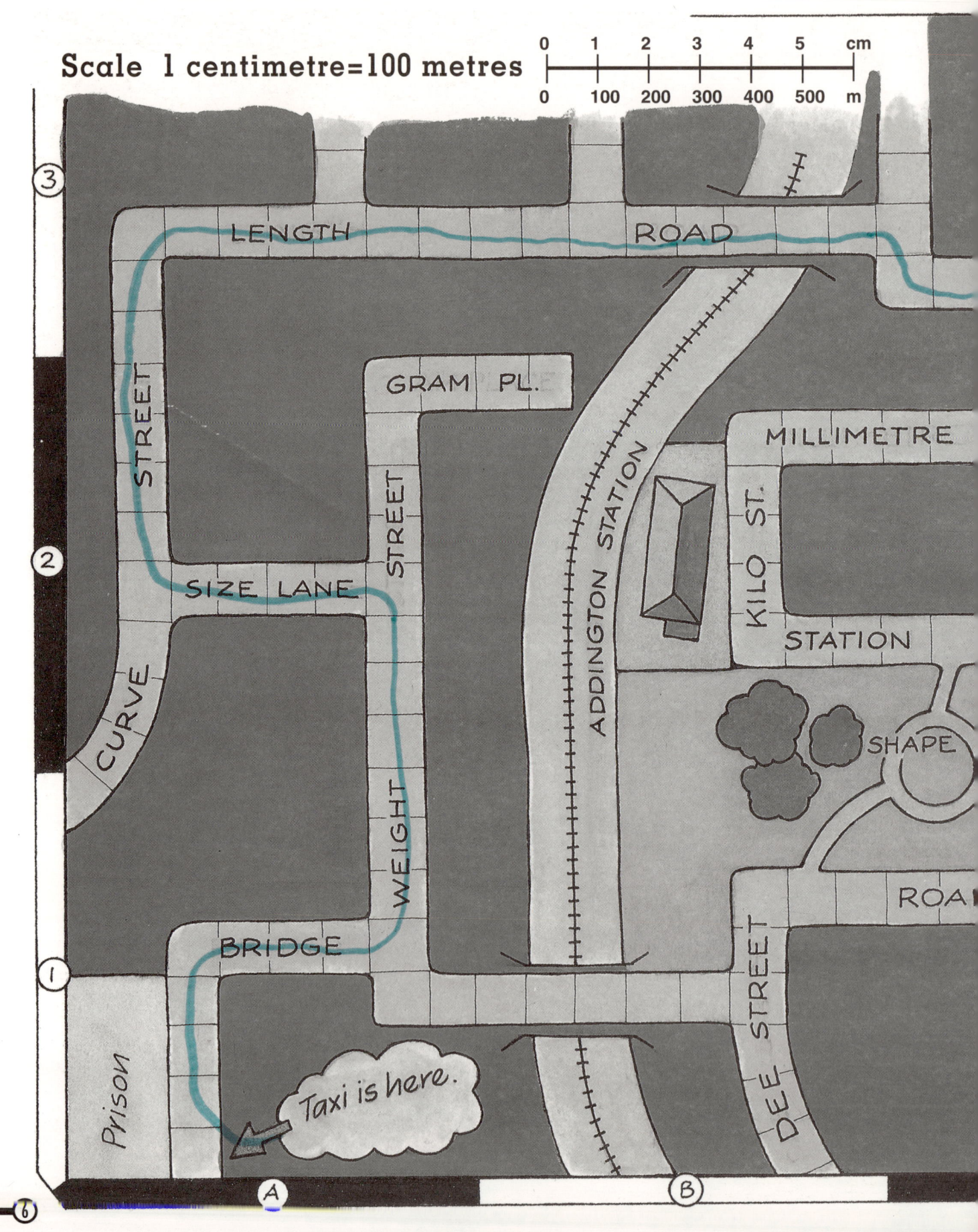

Scale 1 centimetre=100 metres

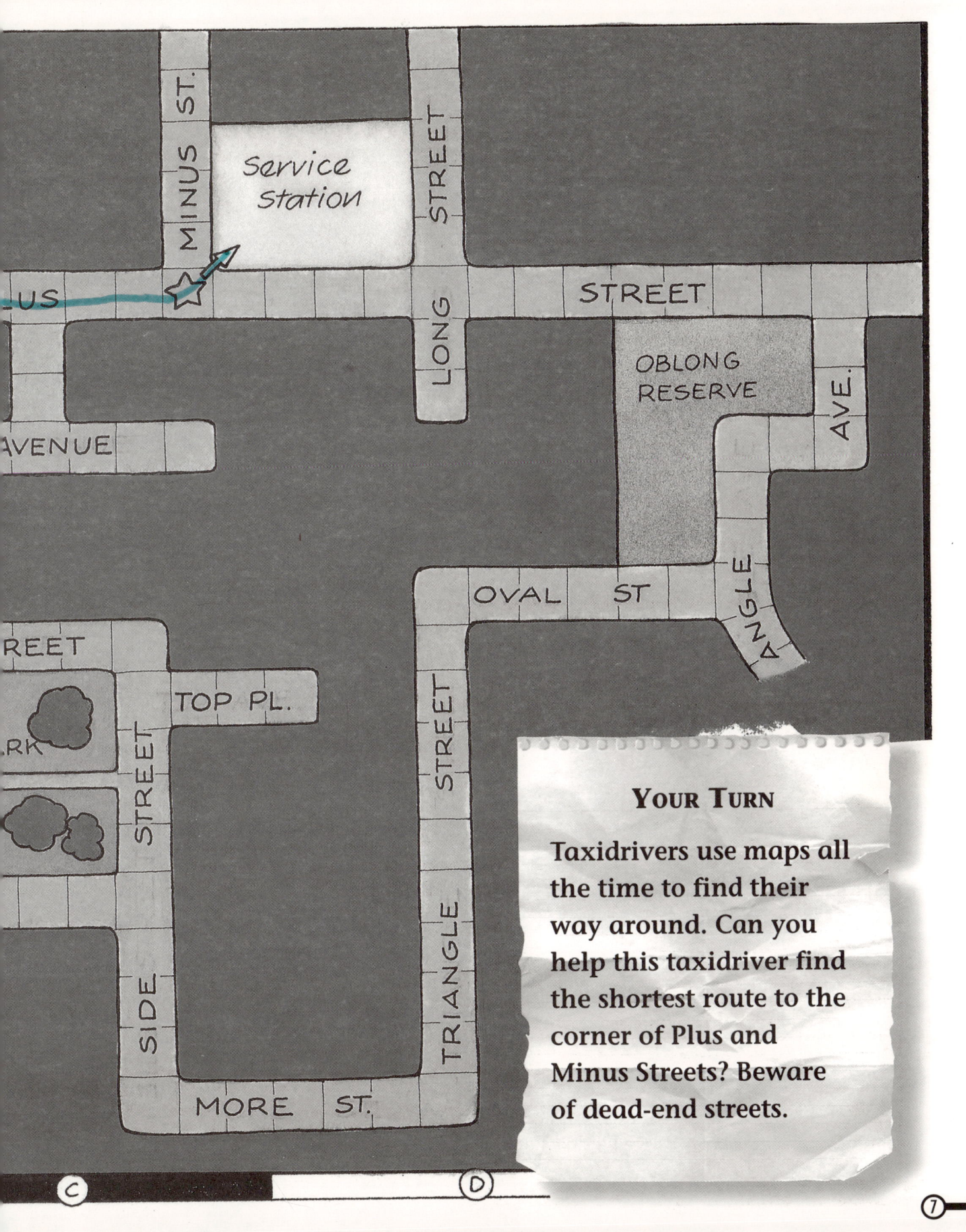

YOUR TURN

Taxidrivers use maps all the time to find their way around. Can you help this taxidriver find the shortest route to the corner of Plus and Minus Streets? Beware of dead-end streets.

At the service station on the corner of Plus and Minus Streets...it's

CHAOS

DIESEL 66 9 per

WHAT?!

Litres 35
Price 68 9
Total

LEADED 70 9   UNLEADED 68 9

COULDN'T BE..?

All the decimal points are missing from the prices!

YOUR TURN

The Number Cruncher has created chaos by removing the decimal points from the prices of the items for sale in the service station.

Can you work out what the price of these products should be?

What might happen if the decimal point became extinct?

In hospitals all sorts of things need to be measured accurately. Temperatures and pulse rates need to be taken to help doctors make decisions about the treatment of illnesses. Medicine must be measured exactly to be correct for the patient's weight, height, age and illness. People's lives depend on doctors and nurses making accurate measurements and recordings.

MEDICAL MATHEMATICS

YOUR TURN

• Spot the mathematics at work in this hospital and make a list of all the ways it's used on this page. Compare your list with a friend's and check again on the next page.

• Ask your teacher to explain how to take your pulse. Count your pulse rate for thirty seconds and record it. Check your pulse rate again after recess. Is it different? If it is, why might this be so?

In Tim's job it's important to know how big a space is. Carpet layers and tilers need to know how big the floor is so that they can buy the right amount of material. To find out the exact amount they need, they calculate the surface area—the amount of space that the floor takes up. The surface area of a room is equal to the length multiplied by the width. It is written as Area = Length x Width (A = L x W).

Will Cal and Dee arrive in time to catch the villainous Number Cruncher?

10 metres

?

10 metres

TILE

1 metre

1 metre

YOUR TURN

The bird's-eye view of the house shows the floor which Tim was going to cover with tiles. Can you help Tim? He needs to know how many tiles to buy to cover the floor of the building, but now that his tape measure has been stolen he can't do it. If you look carefully, all the clues you need to solve the problem are on this page.

Too late again!

The Number Cruncher has managed to steal Tim's tape measure.

I'll just go and get my boogie board.

They are working out the surface area not the surfing area.

Not everyone needs to know surface area the way Tim the tiler did. Some people, such as Sue, just need to know how long something is around the outside —the perimeter. Can you think of times when you might need to know what the perimeter of something is?

MATHEMATICS AT THE EDGE

YOUR TURN

Look at Sue's plans. Can you work out what the perimeter of the room would be? How many metres of cable will Sue need if it is to run around the outside walls?

Do you know where Cal and Dee will find the Number Cruncher next?

And at Hilda's Hardware, it is a busy Friday morning:

I'll just mark and cut this at 1.8m for you.

SPECIAL
2L cans $7
4L cans $14

$11·50

$14·50

$25·00

$3·00 per lin. metre

$6·70

DAISY DUCK VIOLET
BOAT RACE BLUE
LAUGHING BART YELLOW
LUNA PARK ORANGE
PLAY SCHOOL PURPLE
HOT PINK
DINOSAUR BROWN
SMOKY GREY
DEEP DARK RED

1 Litre   1 Litre

10mm brass Washers

3KG

2L

4L

4L

4L

Buying and selling uses the mathematics of money. If you work in a shop, charging the right amount of money and giving back the correct change is very important, but it could also involve a lot more. If you were the manager of a shop such as this one, you would need to pay the staff, borrow money to buy stock, organise stocktaking, order goods and decide on prices. There's certainly a lot of mathematics here.

YOUR TURN

If you were the manager or a salesperson working in Hilda's Hardware, what kind of mathematics might you use each day at work? The illustration might help you with your answer.

You probably didn't realise how much mathematics you do or can find around your home, but you use it all the time. You estimate the temperature of bathwater, tune the video for recording, set the alarm clock, measure ingredients for cooking, judge how much milk you need for a milkshake, consult the timetable for the time of your favourite television program. Of course, you can probably think of many more.

YOUR TURN

How many ways do you use mathematics at home? Why not check it out? Go on a search through your house to discover where the mathematics is and how you use it.

Some people think that mathematics is something you do with a pencil and paper. Sometimes it has more to do with knives and forks. When you cook, you are using mathematics just as a chef does. A chef checks the heat of the oven and the time, to make sure the food is cooked at the correct temperature for exactly the right length of time. Hotplates need to be adjusted so that food is not burnt or undercooked. To follow a recipe properly, scales and measuring cups are used.

In a restaurant, each person at a table must be given the food they ordered—even something as simple as matching orders to people uses mathematics. A waiter also uses mathematics to work out how much the meal cost.

At home, you might need to count the number of people who will be at the table so you can set the correct number of places. You will need to know how many courses will be served so that you can set the correct number of knives, forks and spoons.

There is a lot of mathematics in each mouthful.

Can you map out the trail followed by Cal and Dee using the grid references? Start at the prison. How far did they travel before they caught the Number Cruncher?

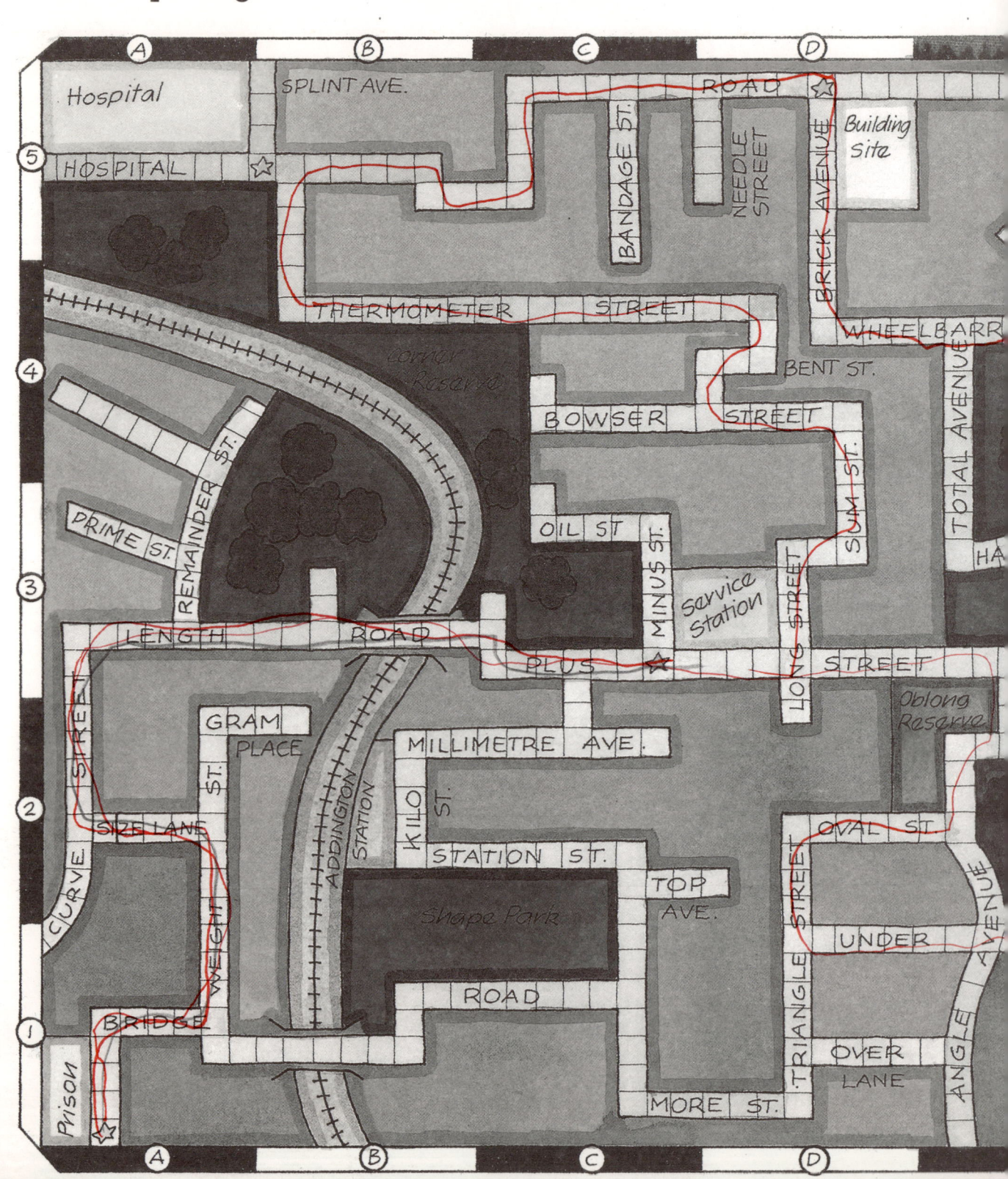

Scale 1 centremetre=200 metres

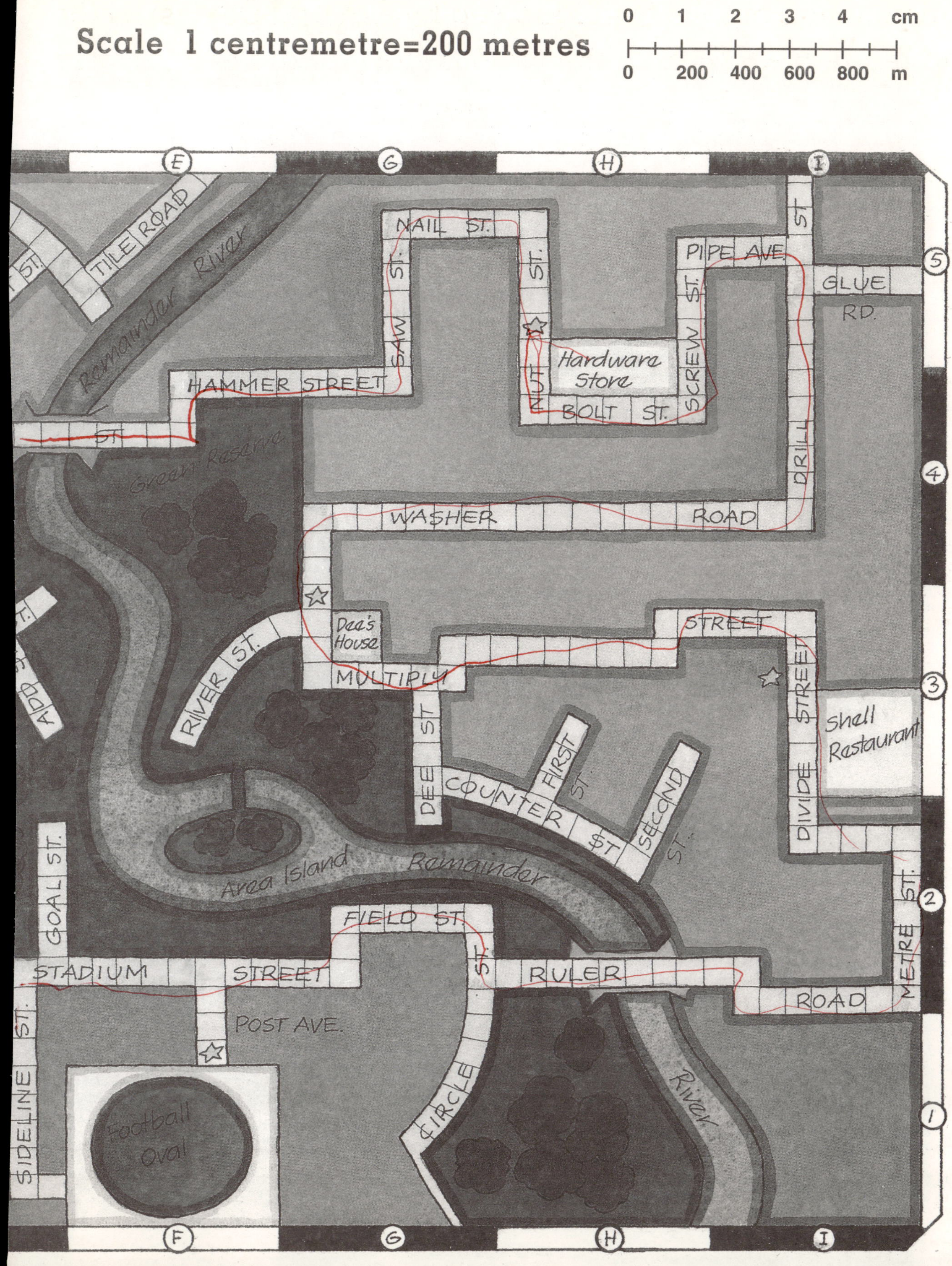
0 1 2 3 4 cm
0 200 400 600 800 m
E
G
H
I
F
5
4
3
2
1
TILE ROAD
Remainder River
NAIL ST.
SAW ST.
NUT ST.
PIPE AVE.
SCREW ST.
GLUE RD.
DRILL ST.
HAMMER STREET
Hardware Store
BOLT ST.
Green Reserve
WASHER ROAD
Dee's House
RIVER ST.
MULTIPLY STREET
DEE ST
FIRST ST.
SECOND ST.
COUNTER ST
DIVIDE STREET
Shell Restaurant
GOAL ST.
Area Island
Remainder
FIELD ST.
STADIUM STREET
RULER ROAD
METRE ST.
POST AVE.
SIDELINE ST.
CIRCLE ST.
River
Football Oval